GENTLE PARENTING

A Biblical Evaluation for Counselors

By Kelli Dionne

ISBN: 9798989125975

Association of Certified Biblical Counselors

As we face the issues of sin and suffering in a broken world, we all need wisdom from God. Thankfully, the Lord has given us all that we need for life and godliness through His sufficient Word (2 Peter 1:3; 2 Timothy 3:16).

ACBC's Truth in Love resources are designed to bring the rich truth of God's character and promises to bear on the problems people face in everyday life. As you walk with others, seeking to minister the very words of God to them, we pray this booklet will be a resource that points you back to His truth and equips you to admonish the idle, encourage the fainthearted, and help the weak (1 Thessalonians 5:14).

Author

Kelli Dionne has her MA in Biblical Counseling from Bob Jones University and is an ACBC certified counselor at Faith Bible Church in Spokane, WA. She counsels women, children, and families, and enjoys teaching counselors and women to love God and His word. She also enjoys counseling couples with her husband, Dan.

As a biblical counselor and an older woman, I am often asked questions about parenting. Last year someone asked me what I thought about gentle parenting and having recently learned about it, my first reaction was less than gracious. Gentle parenting sounded permissive and, frankly, exhausting to me. I am humbled to write this, as when I was a young mom, I was anything but gentle. I had a terrible anger problem. I was easily frustrated with my children as I was enslaved to the praise of man and never wanted to look bad. However, I did look bad though to my children.

Praise God, I have been in a wonderful church where I've been taught the Bible and have a godly husband who helped me repent of anger and parent biblically. I understand why gentle parenting is appealing—its qualities of listening to children and honoring their feelings sound wonderful. Yet, there is value in understanding its origins and principles so Christian parents can discern which, if any, part of it to implement and what needs to be rejected.

Gentle parenting is becoming increasingly popular in our culture and is seen by many as a good method to raise kids. The thinking goes that parents should be gentle...so gentle parenting must be valuable. Yet, it is important to discern things in the context of what God's Word says, and while gentle parenting sounds good, it must be examined and defined from its primary source and contrasted with God's design for parenting. Many are choosing this approach and employing bits and pieces to their parenting methodologies because it sounds gracious and helpful, but its foundational teaching and goals require a biblical critique so that Christian parents can wisely shepherd their children with God's goals as their focus. When it is examined with a biblical lens, it is clear that gentle parenting must be rejected because of its foundation, goals, and methodologies.

Parents have been seeking wisdom for parenting since the beginning of time. Biblical history tells of Adam and Eve and their first children, the patriarchs with theirs, King David with his, and Mary and Joseph with Jesus. Early European history details Kings and Queens with nursemaids and governesses. The Puritans raised their children in an agrarian culture; children working alongside and for their parents, being raised to adulthood with biblical instruction and modeling. Children have been raised in times of difficulty and plenty, with parents and with caregivers. Early in the twentieth century parenting experts taught that children should be matured for life and not coddled. The goal was independence. Then in 1946, Dr. Benjamin Spock published *The Common Sense Book of Baby and Child Care.*[1] This began the trend for more emo-

---

[1] Benjamin Spock, *The Common Sense Book of Baby and*

tion in parenting, more kindness and gentleness. This continued with John Bowlby and attachment parenting in the late 1950s and Penelope Leach's child-led parenting in the 1970s. In the mid 1980s, Dr. Richard Ferber turned the tide with sleep training for infants, and this continued to more authoritative parenting styles through the 1990s.

It is easy to see that parenting methods, like many things, develop and grow cyclically. One generation emphasizes authority, the next autonomy. The current trend in 2024 is gentle parenting. Once again, the pendulum has swung from a legalistic, formulaic style to a more child-centered one. There are many cultural reasons for these trends, with many books and social media influencers touting the benefits of gentle parenting. There are also respected professionals in psychology, medicine, occupational therapies and social work who champion gentle parenting. Christians must not be swayed by so-called experts but be informed by the Word of God toward the goal of raising children who love Jesus Christ and want to glorify Him every day of their lives.

Gentle parenting is seen today as something that is loving, calming, and to some, the best way to raise children. While many sources proclaim the goodness of gentle parenting today, Christian

---

Child Care (New York City: Duell, Sloan, and Pearch, 1946).

parents and biblical counselors must research worldviews and clarify definitions. Gentle parenting is not merely a method, it is an entire worldview. Parenting with gentleness and gentle parenting are not the same thing.

Definition of Gentle Parenting

Gentle parenting is promoted as "an evidence-based approach to raising happy, confident children."[2] There are multiple definitions of gentle parenting, and this is due to its fluidity of interpretation and the individual perspectives on methodology. It is important to begin by looking at the primary source. The method instructs parents to use empathy, respect, understanding and boundaries in parenting children, according to founder Sarah Ockwell-Smith, who studied psychology and was trained in hypnotherapy and psychotherapy. She is a prolific author; her books include *The Gentle Parenting Book*, *How to be a Calm Parent* and *The Gentle Sleep Book*.[3] She is also a teacher, a doula, and is considered a parenting expert by many.[4]

---

[2] Kimberly Zapata, "What is Gentle Parenting?" *Parents*, August 17, 2023, https://www.parents.com/parenting/better-parenting/style/what-is-gentle-parenting/.

[3] Sarah Ockwell-Smith, *The Gentle Parenting Book,* 2nd Edition (Great Britain: Piatkus, 2023); T*he Gentle Sleep Book* (Great Britain: Piatkus, 2015).

[4] Sarah Ockwell-Smith, "About," *SO-S Parenting with*

Traditionally, parenting styles have been described as authoritarian, permissive, and authoritative. Authoritarian parenting values discipline and control, with rules and standards to follow. Permissive parenting is one where children are able to decide for themselves what they would like to do. Authoritative parenting is one with firm limits and discipline, with clear communication and expectations. *Ockwell*-Smith argues that gentle parenting is not permissive parenting. She calls gentle parenting "authoritative parenting" and defines gentle parenting as follows:

> Ethos-a way of being, you might say. It is mindful of current science and child psychology, while remaining respectful of cultural and historical practices of child-rearing. It is a holistic philosophy that considers the emotional, as well as the practical, aspects of parenthood. In a nutshell, gentle parenting is a lifestyle that encompasses both your physical and psychological behavior, not only towards your children but to yourself, too-because parenting should be a dance between the needs of children and parents. With practice, this dance can lead to something quite beautiful, and tremendous growth for both.[5]

Sarah Ockwell-Smith, https://sarahockwell-smith.com.
[5] Ockwell-Smith, *The Gentle Parenting Book*, 1-2.

In *The Gentle Parenting Book*, she teaches the seven C's of gentle parenting: connection, communication, control, containment, champion, confidence, and consistency. These need to be compared and contrasted with biblical truth.

1) **Connection**

» *Gentle Parenting View*: A child's bad behavior stems from lack of connection to parent.

» *Biblical View*: Behavior stems from the heart.

2) **Communication**

» *Gentle Parenting View*: Behavior is communicating physical and emotional needs that must be met; poor communication leads to frustration and disobedience.

» *Biblical View*: James 1:19-20 says that we are to be "quick to hear, slow to speak, slow to anger, as the anger of man does not produce the righteousness of God."[3] And Colossians 4:6 instructs to "let your speech always be gracious, seasoned with salt, so that you may know how to answer each person."

3) **Control**

» *Gentle Parenting View*: Parents give appropriate control to children, reducing the insecurity of no limits while allowing the child to grow and assert autonomy.[7]

- » *Biblical View*: Self-control is a fruit of the Spirit (Galatians 5:22). Children are to develop God dependence not autonomy and submit to authority as their parents must

4) **Containment**

- » *Gentle Parenting View*: Parents need to "contain" their child's big emotions in order to release them; child cannot developmentally regulate feelings.[8]
- » *Biblical View*: Children can learn God's truth and bring big feelings to Him for comfort, wisdom and discernment (Isaiah 41:10).

5) **Champion**

- » *Gentle Parenting View*: Parents must always believe in their children in order for their children to gain courage for life.
- » *Biblical View*: Parents are to sacrificially love their children and teach them wisdom for all of life. God's faithfulness and kindness gives children courage.

---

[6] All Scripture is quoted from the ESV Study Bible.
[7] Ockwell-Smith, 23.
[8] Ibid., 20.

6) **Confidence**

» *Gentle Parenting View*: "Confidence comes from making well-informed decisions and being surrounded by like-minded people-parents who feel the same way as you and raise their children in a similar manner. It comes from building a village of support around yourself and your family. Confidence comes with time and experience , from living in the moment, being mindful of your child's stage of development and taking care of yourself as well."[9]

» *Biblical View*: Confidence comes from abiding in Christ and obeying Him (John 15:1-11). As children learn God's wisdom and ways and follow Him, they will know the "peaceful fruit of righteousness" (Hebrew's 12:11) and this results in confidence in and with Christ.

7) **Consistency**

» *Gentle Parenting View*: Remaining consistent leads to learning and understanding.

» *Biblical View*: Consistency leads to learning and growth and decreases a child's frustration (Ephesians 6:4).

---

[9] Ockwell-Smith, 23.

The Mindsets of Gentle Parenting and Biblical Parenting

A key point is that, in practice, gentle parenting focuses on the emotions of both of the child and the parent. Rather than quick correction of wrong behavior, a gentle parent seeks to understand the underlying emotions driving it. The emotions to understand are those of both child and parent. This is something that, while time consuming, reportedly pays off in the long term as emotional regulation is encouraged and attained. Most explanations speak to raising happy, confident, and secure children as the goal of gentle parenting. Discipline is accomplished through setting boundaries, being consistent, communicating lovingly and clearly, and for many with this view, no physical correction. Ockwell-Smith herself calls this "smacking" in her book.[10]

The best way for Christians to evaluate the mindset of gentle parenting is to begin with God's idea parenting. How does God want his children to parent their children? While the book of Proverbs is filled with practical wisdom for parenting, it may be surprising that parenting commands in

[10] Ibid., 27.

scripture are few. The primary parenting passages are Ephesians 6:4 and Deuteronomy 6:4-9. Ephesians 6:4 says, “Fathers do not provoke your children to anger, but bring them up in the discipline and instruction of the Lord” (also in Colossians 3:21). Deuteronomy 6:4-9 includes:

> And these words that I command you today shall be on your heart. You shall teach them diligently to our children, and shall talk of them, when you sit in your house, and when you walk by the way, and when you lie down, and when you rise. You shall bind them as a sign on your hand, and they shall be as frontlets between your eyes. You shall write them on the doorposts of your house and on your gates.

Hebrews 12:7-11 shows the purpose of discipline:

> It is for discipline that you have to endure. God is treating you as sons. For what son is there whom his father does not discipline? If you are left without discipline, in which all have participated, then you are illegitimate children and not sons. Besides this, we have had earthly fathers who disciplined us and we respected them. Shall we not much more be subject to the Father of spirits and live? For they disciplined us for a short time as it seemed best to

> them, but he disciplines us for our good, that we may share his holiness. For the moment all discipline seems painful rather than pleasant, but later it yields the peaceful fruit of righteousness to those who have been trained by it.

God wants parents to be godly, and to teach their kids about Jesus both in how they themselves live and how they disciple their children. Paul David Tripp, in his excellent resource *Parenting: 14 Gospel Principles That Can Radically Change Your Family*, urges parents to be ambassadors for Christ as they live with and train their children.[11] They must show their children how to please Jesus and how much they need his transforming work in their own lives. This reminds Christian parents that they need to pursue Jesus themselves; confessing sin, (1 John 1:9), being careful with their speech (Ephesians 4), and not giving in to anger (James 1:19-20). They are to love God (Deuteronomy 6:5) and live in a self-sacrificial way, denying themselves and taking up their crosses daily to follow Him (Luke 9:23). Most Christian parents

---

[11] Paul David Tripp, *Parenting: 14 Gospel Principles That Can Radically Change Your Family* (Wheaton, IL: Crossway, 2016).

would testify to the sanctifying work of God in their lives through parenting children! In addition to specific texts of parenting, Christian parents have God's instructions on Christian living, which applies to the way they parent. Before we even talk about mandates for parenting, we must discuss mandates for believers.

As Christians, our purpose in life is to glorify God. 2 Corinthians 5:9 tells us, "We make it our aim to please Him," and 1 Corinthians 10:31 says, "Whether you eat or drink or whatever you do, do it all for the glory of Christ." As God's children, we must bring praise and honor to him every day in every way. This requires us to examine our hearts, our motives, and our desires, and line them up with God's word. This must be applied in how we work, love, serve, and parent. Christians are commanded to walk in gentleness, as well as humility and patience. Ephesians 4:1-3 urges Christians to "walk in a manner worthy of the calling to which you have been called, with all humility and gentleness, with patience, bearing with one another in love, eager to maintain the unity of the Spirit in the bond of peace."

Here we see, as believers we are to walk worthy. What does this mean? It means walking in a proper, godly way, in a manner fitting of the "calling to which you have been called." There is no higher place to do this than with our spouses and children. According to the Apostle Paul we are to walk in humility, gentleness, and patience, bearing with one another in love. Certainly, this applies to the way Christian parents should train their children. It is sinful for parents to use harsh punishment with their children, to shame them or belittle them, to embarrass them or make them fear failing their parents if they make mistakes. Parents are to glorify God before their children, to train their hearts to know God, not cower before Him. According to Ephesians 4:20-32, Christians must depend on the kindness and grace of God to put off their own sin and put on Christ, in their own relationship with God and with others. This is how we are to live whether we are parenting, single or working in a bank or store, and how we function as church members and family members. Why? Because we are called by God and saved by Him; we are not our own, we were bought with a price. God's purposes and plans are supreme.

How does this apply to parenting? We are to be humble and patient with our children, not using corrupting talk, bitterness, wrath, anger, clamor, slander, and malice (Ephesians 4:29-32). Parents are to be tenderhearted and to forgive as they have been forgiven. This is biblically parenting with gentleness. Additionally, Christian parents are to raise their children in the discipline and instruction of the Lord, (Ephesians 6:4). This is where the goals and methods of gentle parenting and Biblical parenting bump into each other.

The Goals of Gentle Parenting and Biblical Parenting

The goal of gentle parenting is to raise children who are happy, confident, and secure. The goal of biblical parenting is to raise children who worship God. Christian parents are to have the same goals for children that God has for them. Happiness, confidence, and security are not bad things, but they must be understood biblically and not according to worldly standards. Truly happy kids are grateful, joyful, and content. Rightly confident kids have a godly ambition, without laziness and demonstrating fear of the Lord. Genuinely secure children demonstrate hearts that are submissive to God. Security in Christ results in obedience and trust. God's goal for children as well as adults is to have a people as his chosen possession. He wants His people to live to glorify Him and make Him known! An important question to ask is: Does gentle parenting accomplish this goal? A careful examination of their definition of these goals is critical.

1) *The goal of happy children*: It is difficult to identify what gentle parenting's definition of happy might be. Is it just the opposite of sad? Happy is a wide term. Of course, all parents want their children to be happy. No one wants sad, miserable children. However, Christians know that a goal of finding happiness in oneself is futile. So, the path to happiness must be clarified. Christians that love the Lord and serve Him with their lives are at peace with God, even while living in a sinful world where things don't always go according to plan. Additionally, there is terrible pain this side of heaven. Yet, Christians can say, "But this I call to mind, and therefore I have hope; the steadfast love of the Lord never ceases, his mercies never come to an end; they are new every morning; great is your faithfulness. The LORD is my portion, says my soul, therefore I will hope in Him." Lamentations 3:21-24. If the goal of life is to be happy without the hope of heaven and God's good plan in view, there can be no true happiness in this life. We are to be happy in Christ and not simply in

our own accomplishments. The Beatitudes teach that to be happy is to be blessed. Christians look forward to the day when all is made right, when every knee shall bow, and every tongue confess that Jesus is LORD (Phil. 2:10-11), when in the fullness of time all things are "united in him" (Ephesians 1:10).

2) *The goal of confident children*: What would a gentle parent define as "confident"? Certainly, being able to navigate life without crumbling emotionally, making good decisions, and knowing themselves well. Christian parents need more clarification. True confidence begins with an appropriate dependence on parents to foster the well-being of children to be able to mature and live on their own. Biblically, Christians are to teach their children well so they can become mature in the Lord. Proverbs 1:7 teaches, "The fear of the LORD is the beginning of knowledge; fools despise wisdom and instruction." The well-being of the child needs to be centered on God's wisdom. Careful thought must be applied to the word confident since Christians are not to be pridefully self-reliant but God dependent. The Christian life is a life lived for God's glory and God's purposes. Maturity is vital, but confidence

that causes a heart to rely on one's own wisdom and desires is what got mankind into problems in the first place. Adam and Eve were given everything they needed to be happy. They decided in Genesis 3 that what they desired would make them happier and this led humanity into sin. Jeremiah 17:9 says that "the heart is deceitful and desperately wicked, who can know it?" A child does not know his heart and following it will not lead to wisdom. Proverbs 22:15 declares, "Folly is bound up in the heart of a child." From birth, children need instruction to reach maturity. They are born sinners and need wisdom from outside themselves. Submission to God's wisdom brings this maturity. Independence potentially builds up self-reliance. We are commanded to be confident in Christ and His finished work on the cross, not in ourselves. This does not mean aspiring to be immature, but to reach Christian maturity through the knowledge of God leading to wisdom, conviction, sacrifice, self-control, and faithfulness. One cannot attain these without learning and depending on Jesus Christ.

3) *The goal of secure children*: Again, this is a term with many implications. In gentle parenting, it refers to the child finding security in

their bond with their parent or having emotional security in themselves. It is true that shy children are easily targeted and hurt by others. Shy children are not always able to flourish socially, and insecure children have trouble maturing to be able to do things for themselves. Being secure isn't necessarily a bad thing but can lead to prideful self-reliance. Maturation is important, but pride is sinful. Pride is often masked behind the euphemisms of confidence and security and can hide a lack of proper submission to godly authorities. Biblical security comes from trust and dependence on the perfect character of God that yields faithfulness and obedience to Him.

The Principles of Gentle Parenting and Biblical Parenting

Gentle parenting seeks to enable children to be happy, confident, and secure through listening well and advocating for children, which are good things when understood rightly. Even though there may be overlap with biblical parenting in certain practices, the two approaches are incompatible fundamentally. The elevation of feelings (emotions) as supreme and a lack of training children to submit to authority are the primary concerns. Gentle parenting advocates seek to enable children to have emotional self-regulation, intimating that wrong behaviors are generated from emotional dysregulation instead of sinful hearts.[12] This means that emotional regulation then is reached when children are listened to and their feelings are honored. They are helped to obey through being understood, according to this view.

Certainly, it is hard for young children to understand themselves and their circumstances. Their need for help is normal. However, gentle parenting advocates say that children need to understand their emotions and parents and other adults need to honor their feelings for this to happen. God says parents are to instruct their children in godliness which includes self-control, kindness, and obedience. Parents love their children well when they understand them, but practically this focus on emotions could potentially fan the flame of disobedience. Secular literature on the method points this out well. An article in *The New Yorker* titled "The Harsh Realm of Gentle Parenting," explains:

[12] To understand the psychological theory that supports this view of humans, see Kyle Gangel, *The "Dysregulated" Nervous System: A Biblical Evaluation of Polyvagal Theory* (Kansas City, MO: ACBC, 2024).

> One of the major themes in "Brain-Body Parenting," and in gentle-parenting discourse generally, is that children don't defy for the sake of defiance, but that their challenging behavior is a physiological response to stress and should be seen as essentially adaptive. The assumption unto itself is questionable: if little Timmy is on the front lawn tossing gardening implements at traffic, his motivations are probably obscurer than stress. This is one of the most confounding dilemmas of parenting, especially as kids exit the toddler stage: that sometimes a child tests or destroys boundaries for the thrill of it. Under the gentle-parenting schema, a child's every act must be seen through a lens of anxiety and threat-detection—which heightens the parent's dual role of child psychologist and emotional-security guard.[13]

Even secularists are questioning if bad behavior is simply physiological stress response. What is causing a child's behavior? Is it a physiological stress response or is the Bible correct in how it describes children as foolish, unwise, and

13 Jessica Winter, "The Harsh Realm of 'Gentle Parenting,'" *The New Yorker*, March 23, 2022, https://www.newyorker.com/books/under-review/the-harsh-realm-of-gentle-parenting.

sometimes rebellious? While the world would not see the root cause as a heart motivated by sin, they can still sense that something is wrong with the gentle parenting explanation of behavior.

The problem Christians run into is that even if a child is over-stimulated or frustrated, it is never an excuse for sin. When we put the primary focus on physiology first, we can miss the heart motive behind mistreating siblings or defying parents. When we do that, we miss the opportunity to teach the gospel of Jesus Christ. Jesus does not merely want our behaviors to change, He wants us to have new hearts. (Matthew 15:18-20; Ezekiel 36:26). The beauty of the power of God is that with a new heart, behaviors change. We can spend tremendous amounts of energy on understanding that it is hard for children to share, but the more important lesson is that children have desires that need transformation.

The Nature of Children

Gentle parenting assumes the inherent goodness of a child, implying that understanding their emotions will lead them to desire and pursue what is good and right. Yet this is patently untrue according to scripture. The Holy Spirit changes our desires through sanctification, and that can only happen after salvation, which is only possible with an understanding of our sin, not our goodness or emotions. Proponents of gentle parenting speak against parenting with shame and guilt and punishing children for how they feel. But what if these feelings and desires are sinful, harmful, or destructive? Guilt is a biblical concept that speaks to our spiritual state erupting from moral wrongs committed by us. Guilt says we have done the wrong thing, and the solution is repentance—not understanding how we feel about what we did. Shame is the embarrassment a child feels for what they did. While biblical parenting should not seek to shame children through harsh words and tearing them down, shame can also be a properly experienced emotion caused by their conscience recognizing a wrong done. We must not neglect teaching children what it means to please God and what wrong deeds are. It is also important to remember that we are training children to be people others want to be around. Helping a child to stop repeatedly doing sinful things brings the joy and peace that they desire. It is loving to train them to say "no" to themselves and think of others first (Philippians 2:3-4).

Submission to Authority

Gentle parenting's ethos collides with biblical parenting in that children need to be taught to obey and submit to authority. Parents can lovingly teach that obedience is a source of joy, not misery. Jesus taught his disciples obedience in John 14. He said, "If you love me, you will keep my commandments." Obedience to Jesus is how Christians show Him their love. Jesus repeated this twice more in John 14, including beautiful promises in response to it: "he who loves me will be loved by my Father and I will love him and manifest myself to him" (v. 21) and "my father will love him and we will come to him and make our home with him" (v. 23). Obedience is how Christians demonstrate love for God. The relationship between obedience and love is a key component of Christian parenting. Children are born sinners who want their own way. Parents are to train them in what pleases the Lord so that they can be truly happy and peaceful.

The world as God ordained it is based on order not chaos. In the time of Judges, everyone "did what was right in their own eyes" (Judges 21:25). There was no submission to authority and the world was dark and chaotic. There was suffering everywhere. It is only when people do what is right in God's eyes that peace is possible. Romans 5:1 says, "Therefore, since we have been justified by faith, we have peace with God through our Lord Jesus Christ." This is eternal peace. The type of peace that gentle parenting is seeking is temporary, and does not necessarily lead to salvation.

Additionally, the Bible helps to inform and correct our emotions, and children need to obey when they do not want to or feel like it. Human beings are emotional, and feelings are not inherently sinful. Emotions are given to people by God to express praise and gratitude to God. They show that humans are created by God and are His image bearers (Genesis 1:26-27). However, these emotions must be informed and regulated by right thinking. Godly thinking comes from God's word, learning to see self and the world from God's perspective. Gentle parenting is a view that celebrates a child's feelings unconditionally yet does not regulate them with biblical wisdom or truth. The foolishness of rebellion is bound up in the heart of a child. A biblical approach allows children to see their sinfulness and need of a Savior who loves them and paid the price for their sin. This is a goal of biblical parenting. Biblically, parents are to strive to know their children and what drives their hearts well, so that they can listen, understand and train with love and grace. It might seem harsh to teach our children that their problem is a sin problem, but this will one day enable them to see their sin clearly and their desperate need of justification. This is where we demonstrate eternal care for the soul of a child, not simply their daily happiness.

Gentle parenting emphasizes that consistency is important in child rearing. Biblical parents need to consistently teach truth to their children in love and patience, showing their children the beauty of the gospel. We were created by God for His glory and purposes and daily we need to teach these principles. When children are led by emotions, there is no consistency because human emotions are intrinsically unstable. They change directions on us like the wind, and when the heart is not governed by the Holy Spirit, it is hard to control them.

Physical Discipline

Gentle parenting denies any value in physical discipline. Ockwell-Smith and others speak a great deal of parent's emotions and triggers stemming from their own childhoods. However, a parent's own abusive childhood does not negate God's directives for training young children. God's word is clear that the rod is a tool of wisdom and love.

Proverbs 13:24 teaches, “Whoever spares the rod hates his son, but he who loves him is diligent to discipline him.”

Parents who focus on honoring and understanding a child’s emotions are putting themselves in situations where it will likely be hard to control their OWN emotions. Ockwell-Smith speaks of the problems parents have when they parent out of their own trauma. She says “one of the most important things you can do as a parent is to make peace with how you yourself were raised.”[14] Referring to the use of “smacking and shaming… hitting a child” as a way of being harshly raised in a parent’s childhood could lead to triggers from the past that could make parenting difficult to do consciously and gently in the present.[15]

There is no doubt that abusive histories lead to abusive parenting without the healing grace of God. Abuse is always sinful, and God hates it. He hates the oppression of the weak (Psalm 72:4; Zechariah 7:10; Psalm 103:6; Psalm 82:3). Children are weak. They need stable love and instruction. They are never to be mishandled or abused. However, Scripture is clear about the value of discipline, including physical discipline, for chil-

[14] Ockwell-Smith., 27.
[15] Ibid.

dren. It is not abusive. Children are to be brought up in the discipline and instruction of the Lord for their own good. This discipline implies training and correction, which also implies that children are not born naturally knowing right from wrong. This is something that they need to learn, as a study of Proverbs teaches their hearts are full of folly. Parents are to lovingly and wisely discipline and train their children with verbal instruction and correction (Proverbs 23:13-14; Hebrews 12:3-11). This is not to punish and shame, but to lovingly train.

Loving Others

It is also important to remember that we are training children to be people others want to be around. Helping a child to stop repeatedly doing sinful things brings the joy and peace that they desire. It is loving to train them to say "no" to themselves and think of others first (Philippians 2:3-4). Practically this can look like getting ready for church on Sunday morning. What should be done with a toddler that won't obey mom in the moment to put their shoes on and join the family in the car for church because they don't want to? Should mom insist or talk? Should said toddler be taught to honor the feelings of others who are waiting or taught that their desires are the most important? Honoring stubbornness can certainly inhibit a parent's ability to remain gentle.

Parents must love their children well by instructing them in love and grace, teaching them how to love and serve others. Focusing on how a child feels may yield frustrating results. We have all seen children in grocery stores or restaurants having tantrums. Honoring a child's feelings in these contexts does not guarantee the behavior will stop. The behavior is coming from a heart that wants what it wants (James 4:1-4). If a child does this in public, it is likely that this is happening at home as well and the parents are exhausted and frustrated. Gentle parenting would emphasize that respect for a child would be the cure, while setting boundaries is the method. How can one set a boundary with this kind of behavior? Instead, one must teach the child that this behavior is sinful, that it does not please God or demonstrate love for others, but only a love of self. The Christian life always involves a degree of denying self (Matthew 16:24; Mark 8:24).

Fostering a child's belief that how they feel is paramount to a good life will only lead to a hard life (Proverbs 13:15). Everyone lives under authority of some kind. Teachers are in authority over classrooms. Children with outbursts of anger now are being allowed to "clear the room" in public schools because teachers cannot express authority. Our jails are filled with people who do not want to live as responsible citizens anymore. This lack of submission is everywhere in our culture today. Everyone is doing what they think is right and what will make them happy, but it is actually making people selfish and unloving. We need the character qualities of self-sacrifice, honor, and service, and training kids to center their focus on themselves and their feelings will not accomplish this.

Cultural Impact

Secular writers, researchers, and professionals are seeing the weakness of therapeutic models and gentle parenting for raising children and solving the problems children experience. Abigail Shrier, the author of *Bad Therapy: Why the kids Aren't Growing Up*, exposes the problems and the exaggerated benefits of therapy for young children.[16] In her book, she clearly reveals

---

[16] Abigail Shrier, *Bad Therapy: Why the Kids Aren't Growing Up* (New York: Sentinel Penguin Random House, 2024).

her opinion of gentle parenting: "Many adhere to 'gentle parenting,' a therapy-infused model that requires parents to give choices instead of orders. (Parents get plenty of orders; children get none.) These parents are 'intentional' about everything. Even before they had kids, they adopted a parenting philosophy. So, does it work? The short answer is no. The longer answer is noooooooooooo."[17]

In her book, she describes stressed out parents and unhappy kids. She relates this to the abundance of therapy available to children in our current climate. Additionally, the gentle parenting model, in her view, is removing parental control and allowing children to have authority that they are not ready for. Shrier continues:

> For thousands of years, until the therapeutic turn in parenting, societies took it for granted that parents' primary job was to transmit their values to their children. And, of course, parents are the ultimate experts on their own values. Once parents decided the goal of child-rearing was emotional wellness, they effectively conceded that the actual authorities were therapists.[18]

[17] Shrier, *Bad Therapy,* 172.
[18] Ibid., 181.

Dr. Diana Baumrind, a developmental psychologist who studied parenting styles, is referenced in Shrier's book. She, coined the terms authoritarian, permissive, and authoritative parenting.[19] Dr. Baumrind believed that authoritative parenting was best as it allowed parents to be loving and relational but still use rules in the home. She insisted that children not be allowed to win conflicts with their parents. Shrier's research led her to conclude "kids are happiest when raised in a loving environment that holds their behavior to high standards, expects them to contribute meaningfully to the household, and is willing to punish when behavior falls short. And it flies in the face of virtually everything therapists and parenting books now exhort."[20]

Conclusion

Gentle parenting has become the new "enlightened" way to parent, but it is fundamentally flawed. We have seen its fundamental beliefs from its founder, Anna Ockwell-Smith, and found much of her worldview to be contrary to Scripture. Christians

[19] Diana Baumrind, "Effects of Authoritative Parental Control on Child Behavior," *Child Development* 37, no. 4 (December 1966): 887-907, https://www.jstor.org/Stable/1126611.
[20] Shrier, 182.

must do all things according to God's word, including marriage, finances, and church life. Parenting is no exception. Gentle parenting denies biblical wisdom. It elevates emotions and a child's individual preferences. It claims that physical correction is wrong, and damages children. Yet God says that it is the tool parents must use to train children (Proverbs 23:13-14, 22: 15, 29:15; Hebrews 12). British Theologian J.C. Ryle reminds parents:

> If you want to make wise decisions for your child, you can't just let them follow their own desires. You need to think, judge, and act for them, just as you would for someone who is weak and blind. But, please, don't let them be controlled by their own unpredictable preferences and inclinations. Their likes and wishes shouldn't be the main focus. They don't yet know what's best for their mind and soul, just as they don't know what's best for their body. You don't let them choose what to eat, drink, or wear, so be consistent and treat their mind in the same way. Guide them on the path that aligns with scripture and what's right, not just what they think they want… Self-will is one of the first things that shows up in a child's mind, and your first task is to resist it.[21]

[21] J.C. Ryle, *The Duties of Parents in Modern English* (Monee, IL; Modern Puritans, 2023), 1-2.

He wrote this over a hundred years ago and it is as important today as it was then. Christian parents must use God's methods for parenting, including physical correction and heart training. This will lead to self-control in body and emotions and a willingness to submit to authorities that God designed and lovingly placed in their lives for His glory and their good. This training includes teaching children that they have a sin problem that only Christ can cure. Parenting is a gospel opportunity! How can a child see their need of a Savior if they don't see themselves as a sinner? Children aren't naturally wise. Adults aren't either. God's word is our source of wisdom. Children need their parents to train them in right wisdom so they can walk wisely, learn of Christ, submit to Him, and have peace with God forever. Godly parenting is gentle, authoritative, and submissive to God's truth in all things in order to train hearts, correct sin, and rejoice in God's goodness. God's plan is a good plan, because it is His.

Biblical Counselors need to be informed about this trend as it is affecting parents and children alike. We must remember and teach that all believers, including parents who are discipling their children, need to be gentle and kind while speaking the truth in love. Gentle parenting reminds us of the value in perceiving how powerful emotions are in young children. Christian parents must remember that when children feel misunderstood, they can understand that as a lack of love. But our culture has swung too far to honoring everyone's feelings about everything, with no regard for truth. We must take great care in combining loving understanding with training children to desire and live by the truth of the word of God. Children who are raised with the expectation that everyone will honor their feelings are being set up for terrific problems in their futures. If everyone they know is only concerned about their own feelings, no one will care about theirs. Feelings DO matter, but they cannot reign supreme. "The heart is deceitful and desperately wicked, who can understand it?" (Jeremiah 17:9). Children need to be trained, loved, and listened to, so they can learn to love Jesus Christ, who is the one who loves them best. It is tragic that they might see Him as harsh because no one cared about how they felt. It would be equally tragic for them to see Him as chaotic because their feelings controlled their lives.

Gentle parenting is not new. It is largely a response to the harsh, legalistic parenting of the previous generation. It is based on man's wisdom as the way to be happy. As stated in Ockwell-Smith's book, it is a "belief system and an ethos." In other words, it is a worldview. As humans, apart from the wisdom of God's word, we are constantly falling into extremes. Christians must live with a biblical worldview, where living in submission to God for His glory and our good is the source of our greatest joy. We must always be gentle in our treatment of others, modeling Christ who did not come to be served but to serve. Parenting must share the gospel of hope for the brokenness of sin as the greatest cure for the pains of this life.

I had to repent of wrong desires and sinful expressions of emotion when I was a young mother. I regret the angry times I had as a young mom, and if I had been allowed to continue ranting away at my children, I would not have honored God or loved my children well. My desire is that Christian parents would learn the biblical understanding of emotions and sin which leads to instructing their children well. This is not gentle parenting; it is parenting gently. Loving our children well and pointing them to life with Christ is the grandest form of discipleship a parent can do.

Biblical Solutions for the Problems People Face

The Association of Certified Biblical Counselors is committed to championing the sufficiency of Scripture for the Church as she engages the problems people face, speaking the truth in love. Christians have the responsibility to bring the truth of God to bear on the problems of everyday life, and to embody that truth in a life of love.

At ACBC, we seek to strengthen the Church to speak the truth in love by providing a quality training and certification process, a global network of like-minded individuals and institutions, and a source of practical and biblical resources for the Church.

In short, we seek to bring *biblical solutions for the problems people face*, upholding that the method God has given to do this is *truth in love*.

Find all our ACBC resources at www.biblicalcounseling.com.